*Do You Have The*
# TIME
*for*
# SUCCESS?

## JULIO MELARA

# Do You Have
# TIME
## *for*
# SUCCESS?

**Global Support Network**
*Tulsa, Oklahoma*

*Do You Have the Time For Success*

Published by Global Support Network

Copyright © 1994, 1997 by Julio Melara

*Cover design and text format:*
Paragon Communications Group — Tulsa, Oklahoma.

# It's Time To Get Off Our Buts and Butts!

# TABLE OF CONTENTS

Introduction

# DEDICATION

I dedicate this book to my mother, Ivonne, whose love and guidance have made me all that I am and all that I ever hoped to be. Because of her, I learned about courage, love, and the importance of working hard. She was always proud of even my smallest accomplishments and constantly challenged me to do my very best. *Through her struggles in life, she taught me that now is the time to pursue my dreams.*

—*Julio A. Melara*

# ACKNOWLEDGEMENTS

The best acknowledgement is always a simple thank you. I feel a deep sense of gratitude to many who have supported, encouraged, and challenged me over the years and during the development of this book.

• To Sherry, my wife, for her unwavering love and encouragement. God has truly given me a gift from Heaven.

• To my sister, Zinnia, and my brother, Manny, for your constant love, interest, and prayers.

• To the boss, William M. Metcalf, my first mentor whose vision and dreams inspired me as a freshman in college. His belief and confidence in me helped me get on track.

• To my dear friends and colleagues in business, especially: Mike Eckstein, LSU Coach Dale Brown, Michael Fleming, John Manzella, Frank Loria, M.J. Gaspard, Jim Hudson, and Terry Jacobson for feedback, encouragement, and always being there to help me.

• To Craig, Glenn, Paul, Woody, J.T. DePaul, Doug, Randy,

and Ray. Thanks for the gift of your friendship. No man could ask for better friends.

• To Kristi Graffeo, Mike Svaoie, Carolyn McLellan, James Cooper Ware, and Julie Bernard for all of your invaluable assistance in the production and development of this book.

• To the people at the News Orleans Publishing Group and WWL Radio—you believed in me, put up with me and challenged me. Thank you.

# FOREWORD

Success! We are all searching for it. But, what can you learn from a 29-year old? The answer is, plenty! Remember the old saying, "Don't judge a book by its cover." In this case, that could not be more accurate, because in this book you will discover wisdom far beyond the years of its author.

You see, the foundation for success is built on learning and assimilating information from all different types of people and sources. Successful people never stop learning or listening. Whether the source is a coach, CEO, teacher, or a young executive, everyone has thoughts and ideas that can contribute to your success. It's only by sharing ideas that you can begin to understand the ingredients of success, not just material success, but happiness in your daily life.

A few years back, I met a young man about to embark on his career. Now, I meet plenty of outstanding young people in my profession, but this one was special. Do you know why? One reason: enthusiasm! I like that because I have always believed that enthusiasm separates those who just want to be successful and those who are successful. I like to be around winners.

Enthusiasm will transform your life because it produces

energy. Think about it. If you are excited about something, won't you be more likely to work harder to attain it? Enthusiasm is like adrenaline, pushing you to accomplish more with greater efficiency.

Dr. Norman Vincent Peale, father of positive thinking, once said, "Enthusiasm is contagious." Not only will it permeate every aspect of your own life, but it affects everyone in your wake. People will be affected by your positive energy and you will see a definite change in their work habits and attitudes.

One word of caution: enthusiasm takes commitment and commitment takes work. You are not going to get out of bed fired up every day, but it is up to you to change your attitude to a positive one. After all, what use do you have for negative energy. It drains you of your most precious resource, your enthusiasm. The side effects of enthusiasm are much more promising. Take a look at a few:

• Enthusiasm reduces and eliminates fear—fear of the unknown and the fear of failure.

• It improves your ability to persuade others. Once you believe, so will others.

• It improves the depth of insight into any situation, job, or problem.

• It adds a more rewarding feeling to your job and accomplishments.

• It puts new creative skills to work.

• It helps others around you to also have more vitality and the feeling of being a winner.

• And finally, enthusiasm will keep you young. After all, it's not your age that counts, it's your attitude.

*—Dale Brown*
LSU Head Basketball Coach

## MENTAL DESSERT

*"Destiny is not a matter of chance, it is a matter of choice. It is not a thing to be waited for; it is a thing to be achieved."*

William Jennings Bryan
(1850-1925)

# INTRODUCTION

In this book I have tried to simplify the meaning of success and identify its principles. Over the years, I have come to understand that everything God created for the human race He made simple; not easy, but simple. Of course as human beings, we have a tendency to complicate matters. I am convinced no matter who we are—black, white, Hispanic, Chinese, male, female, rich, poor, educated, uneducated—we are all looking for the same thing in life: SUCCESS! You name it. From our careers and finances to our families and spiritual life, we all want success in every area of our life.

For as long as I can remember, I have wanted to be successful. When I was 13 years old my mother gave me a little wooden box which I still keep with me today. Written on the outside are the words, "The Secret of Success." When you open the box there is the four-letter word "WORK." From our earliest days, my mom always encouraged my sister, brother, and me to do our best. She instilled in us a good work ethic. Since then, I have been on my journey towards finding success, coming to realize that success is not money, fame, a high position, or anything else except DOING MY BEST. That is exactly what I have set out to do. Who am I? Just a regular person, a salesman by profession, and by nature, a man of action.

Because I wanted to be successful, I set out to talk to people who were successful, read about them, listened to tapes, watched videos, and attended seminars. Why are they successful? What makes them different? Why out of all the people in the world can we classify just a few as successful? How did they get there? On this search I began to see, hear, read, and learn about common characteristics, habits, behaviors, attitudes, and principles in these people's lives. So I began to apply them to my life. Then something interesting began to happen: they actually worked! They worked in my marriage, my relationships, my career, and in every area of my life. One quick example was my work.

# Introduction

During my freshman year in college, I was a courier making $3.35 an hour at a local business newspaper. Four weeks later, the boss gave me a raise to $4.00 per hour. I thought the world was mine. Over the next few years, I worked my way up through the ranks and different facets of the company. During my senior year of college, I wore a suit to the University because I had been promoted and given the opportunity to sell advertising. So every afternoon I rushed out of class to go sell, sell, sell. After working my way through college, I earned $40,000 my first full year. My second year, I earned $70,000, and over the next couple of years, I earned a six-digit income. Now if you would have told me back then that a young Hispanic kid from a lower middle income family, who didn't get the best grades in school, had a stuttering problem, and was raised by his mother would have earned his first half million dollars at the age of 28, I would have told you that you were crazy. Am I rich? No. Am I successful? You bet. Why? Because I decided and committed to always do my best.

Now is the time for you to make the decision to be successful. Make the decision today to have success in your marriage, in your friendships, in your spiritual life, your health, finances, career, and in every area of your life. Do you have the time to be successful? Do you have the time to read this book? I hope so. You see, time is all you have so you better spend it wisely. Time is also an acronym for the four key ingredients in the recipe of success.

T   Talent

I    Information

M   Motivation

E   Enthusiasm

Remember that success is not a destination but a journey. Sit back and enjoy our journey together in the next few chapters.

## MENTAL DESSERT

*"The great thing in this world is not so much where we are, but in what direction we are moving."*

Oliver Wendell Holmes
(1809-1894)

## MENTAL APPETIZER

*Always bear in mind that*
*your own resolution to*
*achieve success is more*
*important than any*
*other one thing.*

*Abraham Lincoln*
*(1809-1865)*

# CHAPTER 1

## Life Is Simple But Not Easy

Over the years I have wondered about this world and about my own life. I have come to the conclusion that life in general is really not that complicated. I don't claim to be the authority on life or a scholar on success but as I always tell people, it is important to remember that experts built the Titanic and amateurs built the ark. By observing, listening, searching, asking, and reading you learn some pretty wonderful things. As human beings we have a tendency to complicate most things, but life really is pretty simple. Take a moment and think about the answers to the following questions:

1. We have thousands of words in the English language. How many letters make up your alphabet?

2. We can earn $12,000 a year, some Fortune 500 companies take in 2 billion dollars a year, and some say the federal deficit could be 10 trillion dollars some day. How many digits make up the numeral system we use?

3. There are thousands of artists who sing everything from country and pop to opera and rock music. People love a variety of musical styles. How many musical notes are there?

4. There are hundreds of colors to choose from when deciding to paint your house. How many primary colors are there?

5. Out of all the decisions you have to make every day, how many real choices do you have to make?

## ANSWERS

1. 26 letters in the alphabet.

2. 10 digits in our numerical system.

3. 7 musical notes.

4. 3 primary colors: blue, red, yellow.

5. 2 real choices.

These are simple answers to what could be complex subjects when you begin to discuss the English language, billions of dollars, or the diversity of music in our culture today.

But look closely at question five and its answer. We all have only two real choices in life. Both of these choices are very simple, except that one choice destroys your hope, dreams, vision, goals, and your life. The other helps you attain your dreams, goals, gives you hope, and enhances the quality of your life on this earth.

The decision all of us must make is either yes or no.

You could choose no. *No,* I really don't have control of my life or destiny. *No,* I really don't have the time to have or pursue goals. *No,* I don't care about tomorrow because I am living just for today. No goals, no direction, no ambition, no vision, NO HOPE! *Que sera, sera.*

Or, you could chose yes. *Yes,* I have decided today to enjoy my life and do the best I can. I have decided to give my best to my family, my work, my country, and to myself. *Yes,* I thank God for the gift of life this day and no matter what happens today, I am pursuing my goals and dreams with all of my heart.

Now, the right choice is obvious. Unfortunately, the no decision is the choice most people choose. Few choose it consciously. Most people have made the no decision subconsciously and don't even know it. By not making a conscious YES decision, people have chosen the no answer. No matter how much they would like to improve their situation or life, it won't happen. Too many people want to change their circumstances but are not willing to change themselves. The foundation for your success begins with making a yes decision that will create the future you desire.

Obviously, our experiences growing up—whether positive or negative — play a major role in the choices we make and attitudes we adopt. However, each one of us at some point in our lives has experienced fear, pain, and failure. All of us have made mistakes, been discouraged, regretted things we have done, been taken advantage of, and have gone through rough and tough times. We have all faced, are facing, and will continue to face adversity in our lives in some shape or form. The key is deciding inside yourself that no matter what happens or comes your way, you are pressing on towards your goal. Happiness and success begin between your ears. Your mind is the drawing table for tomorrow's circumstances.

No one ever drowns because they fall in the water. They drown because they stay in the water. We cannot let the regrets of yesterday, the adversities of today, or the fears of tomorrow rob us of this day. Recognize that adversity has advantages. It reveals the depth of friendships. It will force you to dig for more accurate information. It will help you decide your priorities and what you really believe.

The first step towards success is to decide that's what you want in life, set it as a goal, and decide to pursue it with all your heart. The most wonderful part is that it is never too early or too late to make this decision. Whether it is in your education, occupation, finances, or marriage, it is never too early or too late. TODAY is the day to say YES. Destiny is not a matter of chance, it is a matter of choice. Remember, nothing worthwhile ever comes easy or without a price. Mind management is the key and first priority in improving our lives.

# MENTAL DESSERT

*"The greatest discovery of my generation is that a human being can alter his life by altering his attitudes of mind."*

William James
(1842-1910)

# MENTAL APPETIZER

*There is a time for everything, and a season for every activity under Heaven.*

*Ecclesiastes 3:1*

# CHAPTER 2

# Time Is the Key to Your Success

A ll through high school, my mother constantly told me those were the best years of my life and to enjoy them. Of course, back then all I wanted to do was graduate and be older so I could get a full-time job, make money and buy myself a new car with a hot stereo system. Looking back, Mom was right. Those years were definitely some of the best times of my life. I didn't have to worry about or be responsible for paying a mortgage, any kind of insurance, utilities, or grocery bills. My time was spent figuring out who my date would be that weekend, what I would wear, and how I would scrounge up enough money for gasoline. I really had no clue or understanding of what time it was in my life.

Most of us have this frame of mind. We don't realize

exactly what TIME it is in our life. As human beings, there are different phases of life in which we developed and grow to help us in the next cycle of life. I once heard there are four phases in every man's life. First, man believes in Santa Claus. Second, he doesn't believe in Santa Claus. Third, he becomes Santa Claus. Fourth, he looks like Santa Claus. Now this is not exactly what I was talking about but it does give a good illustration of the fact that there are different cycles we go through in life. This is the case whether you are a 22-year-old college graduate preparing for the business world, an expectant mother having your first child at 32, or a 54-year-old successful businessman who is preparing for retirement. No matter what stage of life you are in, now is the TIME to clearly define what it is you want to accomplish in this life. What could you begin to do today on a regular basis that would make a significant positive impact in your personal life? What about on your business or career?

You have heard it before, time is the most precious commodity we have. This is so true. Time is the only thing that all of us have in equal proportions. Everyone has 24 hours a day to spend, 365 days a year. The problem is that too many people are too busy, get distracted, don't care, or think they can do it tomorrow. One attribute that I have observed in successful people is that they have the ability to make decisions and act in accordance with them in a timely fashion. They are proactive. They don't wait until tomorrow to do what they can accomplish today. They know that lost time is never found again.

Growing up and all through college, I used to think that there was a huge gap or difference between successful people and unsuccessful people. It is clear now that the difference is very small. The only true difference is that successful people have successful habits and unsuccessful people have unsuccessful habits. Successful people are in the habit of time accounting. A business values its money and depends on accounting to show how it is spent. Nothing is more valuable than your time. Yet have you ever made a careful accounting of how you spend it?

People with high personal effectiveness know that it is essential and also a prerequisite to realize what time it is in their lives and that they must manage and master their time in order to have a successful and fulfilling life. This has become a lifestyle habit for them because they understand that if you don't manage your time, you will never achieve your goals.

What does all of this mean? If you have been thinking of going on a diet, now is the time to do it. If you have been thinking about telling your wife or husband how much you love him or her, do it. If you need to apologize or forgive someone, do it today. What about taking Spanish lessons, getting a college degree, cooking classes, vacationing in the mountains, going after a new client, exercising regularly, spending more time with the family, working on your spiritual life, saving money, or calling an old friend or relative. Whatever it is, now is the TIME to do it.

## FIRST THINGS FIRST

How do you do it? By putting first things first. Prioritize what things are first in your personal or professional life. Most of us are so busy that we haven't taken the time to actually sit down, think about, and write down what is truly important to us. What do we really want to accomplish, and why? Most have thought about these things but have never really taken the time to actually decide what we want, write it down, do it and live it. The time to take action is long before one's fortune begins to slip away. Now is the time to access the start of your life in order to determine exactly what action is called for in the next few months and years to help you achieve your goals. If you don't take time to program yourself or your life, life will program you.

Understanding what time it is in your life and that TIME is the key to your success will help you begin to make a life instead of just making a living. Only then will you find the true meaning of success. Let's take a close look at some of the key ingredients that make up the recipe for success in T I M E.

## MENTAL DESSERT

*Never Stop Reaching For More*

*Do more than exist . . . live*

*Do more than touch . . .feel*

*Do more than look . . . observe*

*Do more than read . . . absorb*

*Do more than hear . . . listen*

*Do more than listen . . understand*

*John H. Rhoades*

## MENTAL APPETIZER

*We don't need more strength or more ability or greater opportunity. What we need is to use what we have.*

*Basil S. Walsh*

# CHAPTER 3

# Time

■

**T**is for talent. If you looked up the definition of talent in the dictionary, it would say that it is the natural special endowment, or ability of a person. Now I know all of us have been blessed with a special talent to do something. Often when I speak to different groups and I make that statement, I get some empty looks staring back at me. Most people have a hard time believing that deep within them lies a special talent or ability. The reason is that most people have a low self concept and little or no self esteem. People simply do not like themselves or believe in their ability. Why? Because we have been brought up in a negative society. Pick up today's newspaper or turn on the television and just scan the headlines. It doesn't take long to realize that the news you read, watch, and listen to comes from a negative position. This is the information that is constantly being programmed into our minds. Remember the choice you read about in the last chapter? Each day when you wake up in the morning, you are faced with the choice.

## YOUR SELF CONCEPT AND SELF ESTEEM

Life was meant to be lived in a positive manner. You have the talent and ability within you but you have to believe it. In the Book of Proverbs it says, "As a man thinketh so he is." The mental aspect of your life is more important than your physical presence. All we are, and all we have the potential to become, is nothing more than the product of our thoughts.

Which brings us to our self concept. Self concept can be defined as the way we see ourselves. We have a self concept about the way we dress, drive, speak, what kind of athlete, lover, worker we are. We have a self concept of ourselves about everything we do. This is very important because every battle that takes place in our lives, takes place in our minds. There is a direct relationship between a person's self concept and their performance and effectiveness at whatever it is they are pursuing.

Let's take a salesperson, for instance.

Salespeople always sell in a manner consistent with their self concept. Some salespeople are uneasy about picking up the phone and calling someone. Some may feel uncomfortable asking for the business or negotiating. By becoming more skilled at selling—from setting up appointments to closing—the salesperson will feel more competent, raise their self concept, and become more successful at their trade. This is the trait all top sales people have. They feel and believe they are good at their trade.

If you are a parent, remember that instilling a strong self concept is very important for your child. I still have vivid memories of my mother dressing me for school and telling me how handsome and smart I was. Guess what? I believed it. She constantly told my brother, my sister, and me that we could achieve anything. We believed her because she was our mom and it built a foundation for our lives based on confidence and a high self concept.

At the core of self concept is self esteem. Self esteem can be defined as how much we like ourselves. A person with a low self esteem doesn't like him or herself and a person with high self esteem feels the reverse. How much you like yourself is the key determinant of your performance and your success level in everything you do. This is the reason why it is so important to work on raising and increasing your self esteem.

One of the ways we do this is by watching what we say about ourselves. I hear so many people constantly putting themselves down. I don't have a college degree. I'm no good at . . . . I can't do. . . . I'm Hispanic, black, a woman, Jewish, short, old, etc. They end up speaking and repeating this so much that it becomes reality.

## THE TONGUE HAS THE POWER TO BUILD OR DESTROY

Did you know that the words you speak you believe the most? More than anyone else you believe what comes out of your own lips. This is the reason it is important to put away negativity from our lips. I am not talking about ignoring your weaknesses or denying the obvious. What I am talking about is focusing on your strengths and improving your weaknesses.

For example, if you are overweight don't constantly complain and talk about how fat you are. Instead, talk about your new commitment to exercise and eating right. If you are a salesperson and aren't good at setting appointments over the phone, commit to watching and learning from other salespeople who are good in this area instead of constantly talking about how you're no good on the phone. Talk about your new goal in order to become more proficient in this area.

We have all heard the saying that if you don't have anything good to say about someone then don't say anything at all. The same applies to ourselves. Refuse to release words of defeat, depression, and discouragement. Your words are your life. Get excited over planning your triumphs. Begin to talk about what you can and will do. Your words matter greatly.

## YOUR THOUGHTS MATTER

The first step towards success is to make the right choice. The second step to success is to change the way we think of ourselves and the world around us. Everything starts with a thought. Disease and health, like circumstances, are rooted in thought. Thoughts of fear have been known to kill people. A sour face does not come by chance; it is made by sour thoughts. On the other hand, strong, pure, and happy thoughts build up the body in vigor and grace. All that a person achieves and all that he or she fails to achieve is the direct result of his/her own thoughts. You have been given the ability to succeed and it is within you.

A person can only rise, conquer, and achieve by lifting his or her thoughts. You can only remain weak, negative, and miserable by refusing to lift up your thoughts.

Some of the greatest contributors to society became successful because they refused to listen to the discouraging voices and negative attitudes of others. Pablo Picasso, Albert Einstein, and Abraham Lincoln were all counted out. Either their parents, teachers, or society thought they would not amount to much, but they wouldn't listen. They believed in themselves. I love what Henry Ford said, "Whether you think you can or think you can't—you are right."

All achievements, whether physical, intellectual, or spiritual are the result of our thoughts. Know your gift. Many people around you may never discover you. It is not really important that they do. What is important is that you discover yourself, your gifts, your talents. Popularity is when others like you. Happiness is when you like yourself.

## YOU HAVE TO BELIEVE

Today, begin to change the information being programmed into your mind. Read, listen, and watch programs which will inspire, motivate, educate, and help you grow as a person. Within you is every potential you can imagine if you believe that God has given you the ability to attain whatever you seek. The only real limitations you will encounter are those which you place on your own mind. You will discover that when your talents are set free by your imagination, you can achieve any goal.

The saying, "Anything is possible for those who believe," is so true. You believed you could walk when you took your first step. You believed you could talk when you said your first word. You believed you could learn when you started school. You believed you could succeed and you probably did or you failed because you did not believe.

Think about what you can and will do and then don't just think about it—DO IT!

---

**MENTAL SNACK**

Our happiness depends on using all of our abilities.

---

## MENTAL DESSERT

*This one thing I do,*
*forgetting what is behind,*
*and straining towards*
*what is ahead.*

*Philippians 3:13*

## MENTAL APPETIZER

*The most powerful weapon for achievement is information.*

# C H A P T E R   4

# Time
■

**I** is for Information. Getting the right information, reprogramming your mind and continuing your education is the third key to your success. As you read through this chapter don't just look for interesting information. Examine the areas of your life that have been difficult, limiting, or negative and see how you can begin to change the way you think in those areas. The information you program into your life is vital to your success.

## GETTING THE RIGHT STUFF

So many people in this world have many more problems and challenges than you and I face daily. Whether it's physically, emotionally, or any other problem, they still succeed and prosper. Why? Because they have come to understand that the only barrier between them and anything they desire is the way they think. They understand that their life today is the way it is because of what's been programmed into their mind which produces how they think. So we need to change the way we think and reprogram our minds.

To succeed you need the right information and knowledge. But before we look at how and where to get the right information let us take a close look at how the mind works. You mind is the control mechanism of your entire life. Once we begin to understand what is going on in our mind, we can see how our thoughts operate and we begin to realize that any and all of our goals and dreams are possible. Your mind is a magnificent tool and when you know how to use it, it will be a powerful tool to help you become what you want to be.

For instance, when you misspell a word on paper where does the error come from? Does it come from the pencil you're using, your hands and fingers, or the paper? No. The error comes from your mind. In the same way, a rewarding career, fulfilling relationship, wisdom, good health, sound finances, and confidence all must begin in your mind before they can be expressed through you in the physical world. When you change the information being programmed into your mind, you change your way of thinking and you change your life. You have probably heard different concepts of this before but few people actually know how to utilize and apply the information to produce results.

## PROGRAMMING YOUR MIND

Most people do not understand that we have existing programs in our mental "computer" (our brain) that control the way we get out of bed, how we drive to work, the way we handle our jobs, and the way we respond to everyday activities. People think that most of the activities they do on a daily basis are consciously planned out. This is not true. Almost ninety-five percent of everything we do on a daily basis is habit and is done through preprogrammed subconscious decisions.

So many people say, "I don't like the way things are going." Or, "I don't like this relationship. I don't like the circumstances." Too many people want to change their circumstances but are not willing to change themselves. To change your circumstances, you must first change what is being programmed into your subconscious. Remember your mind/brain works like a computer. Whatever is put into your mind is what comes out. This is one of the most powerful truths on the earth today. As you reprogram your mind and input the right information, you will begin to think differently. Your renewed mind will bring about a different response in your relationships, business, finances, health, and in everything you do. When that happens, you will see new opportunities and other positive results in your life.

## CHANGE IS THE KEY

We have already talked about the negative-filled world we live in. The information being given to us each day through the newspaper, television, radios etc. is filled with negativity and if we don't become good stewards of our minds this is what will be programmed into our minds. No one has put it better than Paul the Apostle when he wrote, "Do not be conformed to this world but be transformed by the renewing of your mind." To paraphrase Paul: do not conform, do not listen to the negativity, discouragement, and junk in this world but be transformed (change the way you think, change the information being programmed into your mind), by the renewing of your mind. The word "transform" literally means metamorphosis, a complete change in form. We must change the information being programmed into our minds.

Many people resist change because they have tried and

failed or because they don't want to get out of their comfort zone. But a change or a mental exchange must take place. You have to remove what I call "stinking thinking" and replace it with right thinking or new programs. If you resist change because you think people or circumstances are controlling you—you are wrong! You have your finger pointed at everyone else instead of yourself. You are the gatekeeper of your mind. This is the bottom line: if you change the information being programmed on the inside, the outside circumstances will take care of themselves. When you plant the proper seed (information) in your mind, you will find the fruit you have been waiting for all along.

## FEED YOUR MIND THE RIGHT INFORMATION

From elementary and junior high to high school and college most of our mental development and study comes through formal education. Unfortunately, this is the end of most people's education when it really should be the beginning. Too much of our society is getting its information and education from television. Continuing surveys indicate the following:

Television is on in most home some 30-45 hours per week.

Senior citizens spend an average of 7 hours a day watching television.

Kids average three to four hours a day watching television.

We are spending less time doing serious reading, exploring and studying new subjects, or thinking analytically. If you are getting the bulk of your information and education from television, your chances to be successful in life are slim.

Take for instance a Chief Executive Officer. The average CEO in America spends less than five hours per week watching television. Is this a coincidence? No! There is a direct correlation between being successful and watching television. Mental development, study discipline, and continuing education are vital to transforming our minds and these should not be coming from television. Earlier I said that successful people are proactive people and proactive people figure out ways to discipline themselves to increase their knowledge and their education.

There is no better way to inform and expand your mind on a regular basis than to get into the habit of reading good books and literature of substance. After graduating from college, most people never pick up another non-fiction book again. They will read romance novels, magazines, the newspaper, local tabloids but never pick up a non-fiction book. Have you heard that the person who doesn't read is no better than the person who cannot read? Well this is true. All leaders are readers. Where do you start?

## START READING WHERE YOU ARE

Begin by reading one non-fiction book a month no matter what the subject—sales, relationships, effective communication, organization, time management, leadership, management, history, etc. Commit yourself to reading. It will expand your horizons, understanding, and awareness in various fields and subjects. You will begin to learn more and program new information into your mind and this will help you grow. The more you know, the more you build your self esteem and become more confident. Information breeds confidence. After you have been reading a book a month move to reading two books a month, then three. If you don't know of any good non-fiction books, there are some I highly recommend at the end of this chapter.

Another way to make good use of your time is to listen to cassettes in the car. We spend hundreds of hours a year in our cars. Why not use this time to learn? As someone once said, "Make your car a University on Wheels." If you commit to utilizing your spare time to learn, you will maximize your time to program your mind with the right information you need to grow and succeed.

Still another way to get information is to simply ask! There are people who cross our paths daily who have the experience and knowledge we need. They can be excellent information sources. Unfortunately, some people are afraid to ask simple questions for fear of coming across as incompetent. Others don't want to ask because they are afraid they might not get the answer. On the contrary, most of the time, when you ask questions that show you have a desire to learn more, people will give you the answers or information you are looking for.

Yet another way to acquire information is to invest in going to workshops, college courses, training sessions, or seminars which pertain to a subject matter that you are interested in or will help you perform your job better. The greatest investment you can make is not in real estate, the stock market, or mutual funds, but in your mind. Andrew Carnegie said, "I believe the true road to permanent success in any life is to make yourself master in that life." You cannot become master of anything in life until you commit to learn as much as possible about that subject or field. Your commitment to acquire knowledge and information will determine just how far and how much you can accomplish.

One last word on information. Information without application is USELESS. Someone once said, "Knowledge is power" and that is true only if we use the knowledge we acquire. Commit yourself to grow and learn. Too many people spend their entire lives defending what they know, rather than seeking to grow.

## RECOMMENDED READING

*How to Stop Worrying and Start Living*
by Dale Carnegie

*How to Win Friends and Influence People*
by Dale Carnegie

*How to Master the Art of Selling*
by Tom Hopkins

*The Greatest Salesmen in the World*
by Og Mandino

*Move Ahead With Possibility Thinking*
by Dr. Norman Vincent Peale

*The Power of Positive Thinking*
by Robert Schuller

*Live Your Dreams*
 by Les Brown

*The 7 Habits of Highly Effective People*
by Stephen R. Covey

*Positive Thinking Every Day*
by Dr. Norman Vincent Peale

## MENTAL DESSERT

*"Knowledge is knowing where to get information when you need it and then acting on it."*

## MENTAL APPETIZER

*To stay motivated,
we must constantly
fight ourselves.*

# CHAPTER 5

## Time

**M** is for motivation. What is motivation?

In its simplest form, motivation is a need or desire that causes a person to act. Different things motivate different people. Some people are motivated by money, some by fear of failure, others by a desire to succeed or prove something. There are probably hundreds of other things in life which motivate people. Abraham Lincoln once said that people are motivated by the lure of wealth or by the fear of being fired at least some of the time.

Regardless of what motivates or doesn't motivate you at this stage in your life, there are a couple of things which are vital to your success. First, only you can motivate yourself. Secondly, within each human being there is a failure mechanism and a success mechanism. The failure mechanism within each one of us is the comfort zone. Unless you step out of your comfort zone, you will never be able to grow, develop, and succeed at anything. It's been said that the comfort zone is the killer of human potential and it is! The reason people don't like getting out of their comfort zone is primarily because of fear of failure. The freedom to step out of your comfort zone even if you fall down or fail at something is vital if you are going to succeed. Successful people are not afraid to fail and are willing to take risks. They understand the law of failure is one of the most powerful of all the success laws because you only really fail when you quit trying.

On the other hand, the thing that triggers the success mechanism in human beings is a set of goals. Unfortunately, most people don't have goals. Some people have goals but they're not written down. They don't realize that these aren't goals but wishes. You can wish until the cows come home but nothing will happen unless your wish becomes a goal. Only a small percentage of our population have goals which are written down and are specific.

## WHAT ABOUT GOALS?

The purpose of goals is to focus our attention. The mind will not reach toward achievement until it has clear objectives. This is when the success mechanism is turned on, the current begins to flow, and the power to accomplish becomes reality. Goal setting is the strongest human force for self-motivation. Unfortunately, too many people take goal setting for granted.

There are four primary reasons why people don't have goals.

1. They simply don't realize the importance of goals.

2. They don't know how to set goals.

3. Fear of failure.

4. Fear of rejection.

If you fall into any of these categories, today is your day. Get a pencil and pad out because I am going to show you a simple goal setting methodology which is solid and works. Before we get into goal setting, let me share with you what some successful people have said about goals.

*"A goal is nothing more than a dream with a time limit."*
Joe L. Griffith

*"People with goals succeed because they know where they are going."*
Earl Nightingale

*"There is no achievement without goals."*

Robert J. McKain

*"If you don't know where you are going, how can you expect to get there?"*

Basil S. Walsh

*"No one ever accomplishes anything of consequence without a goal."*

Paul Myer

We need goals to give us a purpose and create excitement in our lives. I have personally done extensive study on this subject. One of the most important studies I came across was of alumni ten years out of Harvard University to find out how many were achieving their goals. An astonishing 83 percent had no goals at all. Fourteen percent had specific goals, but they were not written down. Their average earnings were three times what those in the 83 percent group were earning. However, the three percent who had written goals were earning ten times that of the 83 percent group. People who write down their goals (objectives) achieve the most of all. Why? Because we function like a bicycle: unless we are moving forward toward an objective, we will fall and fail. That is exactly what a goal is—an objective. Picture a basketball game without goals. Without a basketball goal, there would be chaos on the court, no opportunity to keep score, and no one would know who won or lost. With goals in place, the players have a reason to be there to compete and excel. That is why in all sports you have goals. Goals are benchmarks for success.

J.C. Penney, founder of the retail clothing store, expressed the same thoughts in a more powerful and precise language when he said, "Give me a stock clerk with a goal, and I will give you a man who will make history. Give me a man without a goal and I will give you a stock clerk."

## DEVELOPING SOUND GOALS

There isn't just one correct way to set goals but there are many wrong ways. First of all, your goals must be consistent with your personal and professional values and priorities. The following criteria will help you in the process of goal setting:

1.  **Goals Must Be Demanding.**

    A valid goal requires your best effort if it is to be motivating and rewarding.

2.  **Goals Must Be Realistic and Achievable.**

3.  **Goals Must Be Measurable So That You Can Know When They Have Been Accomplished.**

**4. Goals Must Have a Timetable or Deadline.**

**5. Goals Must Be Written Down.**

If you don't write them down you don't have goals. When you write down your goals they become a commitment. They become something concrete that you're committed to achieving. Another reason it is important to have them written down is because "out-of-sight is out-of-mind." One of the most common reasons for failing to reach an objective is losing sight of the goals. Having your goals written down and reviewing them during tough times will remind you why you must and will persevere. On the other hand, there is nothing which builds your self esteem more than when you write down your goals and check off the goals you have accomplished. This builds confidence and makes you ready for your next challenge.

Now, take out a piece of paper. At the top of the sheet, write, "My Lifetime Dreams and Goals." Write down in detail everything you would like to become, do, or have during your lifetime. Dream your dreams on paper.

Take out another sheet of paper and write down, "My Twelve Month Goals." Your twelve month goals should be broken down into these three major areas:

I.   **Personal Goals**

II.  **Professional Goals**

III. **Self Development Goals**

Under each one of these major areas you can list your sub-categories. Personal goals deal with your family, finances, spiritual life, health, marriage, home, or social life. Professional goals deal with your current position, getting a raise, a promotion, starting your own business, acquiring a new top account, etc. Self development goals deal with improving the quality of your life. These are the things you can do to improve yourself physically, spiritually, and intellectually. You should have at least three to five goals under each category.

Now take out one more sheet of paper and write "My Thirty Day Goals and Action Plan." Here is where you begin to map out your daily and monthly routine which will help you accomplish your major goals. Write down the most important things you will do in the next 24 hours and then the next week. The secret of your future is hidden in your daily routine.

## AIMING HIGH

One last word on your goals—always aim high! Over the years I have learned that high expectations produce high results. Medium expectations produce low results. Low expectations produce no results. Your determination, diligence, and persistence will help you achieve everything you want to achieve in this life. In the end, your persistence will be the key factor in determining your success. Nothing in this life that is worth anything comes easy. Persistence will be your ability to face adversity and defeat from time to time without giving up—to push on in the face of great difficulty. Persistence means taking pains to overcome every obstacle, and to do what is necessary to reach your goals. Set your goals and go for it today!

## MENTAL DESSERT

*"My mother said to me, 'If you become a soldier you will be a general; if you become a monk you will end up as the pope.' Instead, I became a painter and wound up as Picasso."*

*Pablo Picasso*
*(1881-1973)*

## MENTAL APPETIZER

*The real secret of success is enthusiasm. yes, more than enthusiasm, I would say excitement. I like to see men get excited. When they get excited, they make a success of their lives.*

*Walter Chrysler*
*(1875-1940)*

# CHAPTER 6

......................................................................

# Time
■

**E** is for Enthusiasm!

Enthusiasm is the priceless quality that makes everything difficult. The men and women who achieve the most are invariably inspired by enthusiasm. They approach life, its opportunities, and its adversities with this vital characteristic. Enthusiasm is a powerful force that is contagious.

Words synonymous with enthusiasm are passion, fire, or zeal. My favorite is passion. Someone who is enthusiastic or passionate about something is obsessed with it. You will never have significant success with anything until it becomes an obsession with you. An obsession is when something consumes your thoughts and time.

You will only be remembered in life for your obsessions—Thomas Edison, inventions; Colonel Sanders, fried chicken; Henry Ford, the automobile; Billy Graham, evangelism; the Wright brothers, the airplane; Walt Disney, Disney World; Dr. Norman Vincent Peale, the power of positive thinking. Each of these people had a passion for their mission and goal in life.

## ENTHUSIASM—IT'S POWERFUL

Ralph Waldo Emerson said, "Nothing great was ever achieved without enthusiasm." I wish I had come up with that quote because it is simple, yet powerful. Enthusiasm is a powerful force which flows out of a person's inner being. The energy it produces can and will produce positive results at every level.

I learned the power of this quality in 1988 when I worked in radio sales at WWL Radio. My first year in sales, I really didn't know that much about radio jargon, number computations, and a lot of other things but I was excited about my product, helping clients, making money, and the life I was living. In the next two years, I became the top producer at the station, breaking sales records and still working hard to learn more about radio, selling, communicating, giving effective presentations, and other skills required to be successful. The one key ingredient I always had was enthusiasm. I cannot tell you how many clients had bad days and would call and ask me to stop by. They always enjoyed my visit and the result was usually a sale for me. Why? Because all people enjoy being around enthusiastic, upbeat, positive people.

One of the primary reasons why enthusiasm is so powerful is because we live in a negative world and people are starving for good news. People are looking for other people who are passionate about their careers and their lives. Does this mean that people who are enthusiastic never get down. No! What it does mean is that people who are full of enthusiasm never let the cares or adversity of life get them down. In the midst of every challenge or problem they look for opportunities, solutions, and they have hope and faith, knowing that in the end everything works out. It always does.

## ENTHUSIASM PRODUCES WINNING END RESULTS

One of my favorite stories on enthusiasm is when Vince Lombardi took over the Green Bay Packers in 1959. The previous year the Packers had lost 10 out of 12 games and were at the bottom of the league. When the players came to camp in June of 1959, they were greeted by the new coach, Vince Lombardi.

According to an article in *Guideposts Magazine*, the new coach said, "Gentlemen, we are going to have a football team. We are going to win some games. Get that!"

Now, how were they going to do that? He said, "You are going to learn to block, run, and tackle. You are going to outplay all the teams that come up against you." Then he threw the clincher! He ordered, "You are to have confidence in me and enthusiasm for my system. Hereafter, I want you to think of only three things: your home, your religion, and the Green Bay Packers. Let enthusiasm take hold of you!"

## ENTHUSIASM HELPS YOU PERSEVERE

It was the power of enthusiasm that enabled Noah Webster to spend 36 years on his dictionary. The irresistible power of enthusiasm saw Thomas Edison endure 10,000 defeats before he perfected the incandescent lamp. Your enthusiasm will help you get over the humps of life because it is an attitude which works.

## PROTECT YOUR ENTHUSIASM

Your enthusiasm for work, life, family, etc. is the most precious ingredient in any recipe for success. Guard it with all of your heart and mind.

*Time*

Our world is filled with enough negativity, doubt, depression, disbelief, and failure. In order to protect our enthusiasm and make sure our fire is lit constantly, there are a few areas in our lives which we must guard closely. These are not in any specific order but you must remember them.

- The *family* members we listen to.
- The *friends* we have and company we keep.
- The *conversations* we have daily.
- The *thoughts* we entertain.
- The *books* we read.
- The *television* programs we watch.
- The *music* we listen to.

Family—sometimes your own blood can hurt you more with their words than total strangers. If you have any family members who consistently cut you down and put you down, don't listen to them. Stay focused on your own goals and agenda. Furthermore, if they don't live in the same house, be cautious of the time you spend with them.

Friends—when I was fifteen years old one of my very best friend's father looked at me and said, "Show me who your friends are and I will tell you what you are going to be." I never knew exactly what that meant until I graduated from college. In its simplest form: hang around bums and you will be a bum; hang around people who are negative and you will be negative. Remember that misery loves company. Hang around people who are successful, excited about life, and enthusiastic and you will be successful, excited about life, and enthusiastic. Remember, we will always be a product of our environment and the people we spend time with. There are four types of people in our lives. Those who add, subtract, multiply, and divide. It is up to you to remove the people who subtract and divide from your life. Get closer to those who add to and multiply your life — people who encourage you, push you, and challenge you!

## ENTHUSIASM CAN BE ROBBED SUBTLY

In American culture one of the most insidious robbers of enthusiasm is television. Every night a large portion of our society watches the ten o'clock news right before they go to bed. What is on? Negative headlines lead the news— murder, rape, unemployment, war, suicides, etc. These are the last images being programmed into the minds. Do you remember earlier you read about how the mind works and is programmed? These depressing and negative images filter into the subconscious and are filed away. People wonder why they had bad dreams or didn't sleep well and wake up not feeling good about life or going to work. We must be good stewards of our minds because everything, whether positive or negative, has an effect on us.

## MORE ON PROTECTING YOUR ENTHUSIASM

There are two times of the day in which our minds are more open to creativity and absorbing information. Our minds function at their best early in the morning and late at night. This is because our minds are clear, free of clutter and distractions. If you want to keep the fire of enthusiasm burning, you must make the following routine a way of life.

Every morning when you wake up, commit the first 30 to 60 minutes to reading. I am not talking about reading the newspaper but reading something positive every morning. Whether it is spiritual, inspirational, or motivational, use the first 30 to 60 minutes of your day to feed your mind positive information. Just as it is important to stretch and warm up the muscles before exercising, it is just as critical to do the same for our minds. Plant seeds in the fields of your mind, which will produce a harvest. This exercise every morning will start off your day on a good note. Your frame of mind is already programmed in a positive manner and you will be prepared to face the challenges of the day.

At night let the last thing you program into your mind and what comes out of your mouth be something positive. Instead of watching TV right before going to bed, read something that will help and challenge you. Let the last words out of your mouth be, "I love you, honey" to your spouse, or "You are going to do terrific on your test tomorrow" to your son or daughter. Put this program to practice every day and it will change your life forever.

Remember to take hold of, protect, and cultivate enthusiasm and perseverance. Every tomorrow has two handles. You can take hold of the handle of anxiety or the handle of enthusiasm. I say, choose enthusiasm.

## MENTAL DESSERT

*"A man can succeed at almost
anything for which he has
unlimited enthusiasm."*

*Charles Schwab*
*(1862-1939)*

## MENTAL APPETIZER

*If one advances confidently in the direction of his own dreams, and endeavors to live the life which he has imagined, he will meet with a success unexpected in common hours.*

Henry David Thoreau
(1817-1962)

# CHAPTER 7

# It's Up to You

**W**alter Cronkite once said, "I can't imagine a person becoming a success who doesn't give this game of life everything he's got."

At the beginning of this book I told you that the first step towards success is to decide that's what you want in life. Many people dream about becoming a success but few do what it takes to turn their dreams into reality. They see their lives and jobs as nothing more than work, and wonder why they don't succeed. To win in this game of life, you must be dedicated. To be dedicated means to give oneself completely to a goal. This takes self discipline.

## WHY SELF DISCIPLINE?

People who achieve success share this one thing called

self discipline. Self discipline is the foundation of self improvement. It channels your resources of time, energy, and money into the habit of learning and growing towards something new and better everyday. To develop self discipline is to take possession of your mind with such strength that your emotions and appetites are brought under control. That is really what you do to achieve self discipline. You tell yourself, "I control my mind; I control my body; I control my actions." This is self discipline. It's doing what you know you should do when you should be doing it.

Think about your life now. Are you disciplined? Are you truly dedicated to your goals? If not, are your half-hearted ways of reaching success getting you anywhere? If the answer is no, why not improve your chance for success through dedication and faith?

Realize that people who are not dedicated to anything don't advance, change, or grow while people who are dedicated to their goals literally get transformed by success. Success changes and transforms people. I have learned that as people continue to grow and become more successful, they often discover that giving of themselves is more thrilling than getting. The concept of helping others succeed has been the key message of successful people since the beginning of time. Inventor Thomas Edison once told a reporter, "My philosophy of life is work, bringing out the secrets of nature, and applying them for the happiness of man. I know of no better service to render during the short time we are in this world."

Andrew Carnegie once said, "No man becomes rich unless he enriches others." Realize the time you are being given on this earth is a journey to be enjoyed and shared. Too often, instead of living one day at a time, we get wrapped up in thoughts of tomorrow. We always complain that our days are few, but we act as if there is no end to them. We think the only reason for our existence is to get to the next destination when it isn't. To comprehend the difference between your journey and destination, you need to understand what Chris Neck meant when he wrote the following:

> A young man searches for happiness:
> In addition to searching for truth.
> He tries to discover true peace,
> During the early days of his youth.
>
> He climbs the highest mountain,
> He covers uncharted ground,
> Expending much of his energy,
> In hopes that the answer will be found.

After all the stones are turned over,
And the searcher has slowed stride;
The older man finally realizes,
That the answer was always inside.

As we live each day to the fullest,
We must not forget to recall;
"It is better to have tried and failed,
Than to not have tried at all."

Now that our journey is almost over,
The answer is a revelation,
This significance is the JOURNEY,
And not the destination.

## THE TRUE JOY OF LIFE IS THE TRIP

Enjoy the journey. "Relish the moment" is a great motto especially when coupled with Psalm 118:24 which says, "This is the day the Lord has made; let us rejoice and be glad in it." It isn't the burdens of today that drive us crazy. It is the regrets of yesterday and the fear of tomorrow which rob us of today.

Start today to put the key ingredients of success to work for you.

## REALIZE

You have the Talent.

(All the ability you will ever need is within you.)

## READ AND RETAIN

Information is vital to your success.

(All leaders are readers.)

## REMEMBER

Your Motivation.

(Goals will keep the fire of motivation burning.)

## RELEASE

Your Enthusiasm.

(Nothing is as contagious as enthusiasm.)

## A FINAL WORD

As I conclude this book, I want to repeat the statement you read at the beginning that said, "Life is simple, but not easy." The concepts I have outlined for achieving success are simple but definitely not easy. I am personally challenged every day of my life with much of what I have shared in this book. To believe in myself when I have failed, to be disciplined in acquiring information, to stay motivated and focused on my goals, and to be enthusiastic every day of my life in the midst of this negative world is the central challenge in my life. But by taking up the challenge and struggling with it every day I have found a deep sense of self worth and a fulfillment that has given greater meaning to everything in my life. I believe that you too can find fulfillment and meaning if you will simply take the TIME for success. I urge you with all my heart to begin today. After all, TIME is ticking away!

## MENTAL DESSERT

*"It is not death that a man should fear, but he should fear never beginning to live."*

Marcus Aurelius

*It's
Time
For
Action!*

## Also available from Julio Melara

• Keynote For Success educational and innovating workshops customized for companies and organizations.

• Motivational Quote Booklets:
  • Time To Win
  • Time for Action
  • Time Out
  • Time To Smell the Roses
  • Time To Think

  • Time for Success Audio Cassette
  • Time for Success Calendar
  • Time for Success Memo Cube Pads
  • Time for Success T-Shirts

# NOTES

# NOTES

# NOTES